CONTEMPORARY OBJECT LESSONS FOR CHILDREN'S CHURCH

LOIS EDSTROM

BAKER BOOK HOUSE

Grand Rapids, Michigan 49506

ISBN: 0-8010-3432-9

Twelfth printing, August 1995

Printed in the United States of America

CONTEMPORARY OBJECT LESSONS FOR CHILDREN'S CHURCH

Contents

Preface   7

1   Choosing What Is
     Best   9
     Choices

2   Behind and
     Ahead   11
     Repentance

3   The Other Side   13
     God's Faithfulness

4   Living Power   15
     God's Power

5   Unlimited
     Possibilities   17
     Overcoming Handicaps

6   New Discoveries   19
     Knowing God

7   Button Up   21
     Union

8   Sweet as Honey   23
     Kind Words

9   Under Cover   25
     Forgiveness

10   Sing a Song   27
     Thankfulness

11   Are You Positive?   29
     Positive Attitude

12   Listen Carefully   31
     Hearing God's Word

13   Threefold   33
     The Trinity

14   Something Extra   35
     Eternal Life

15   One of a Kind   37
     Our Uniqueness

16   A Good Flavor   39
     God's Love

17   Grow and
     Overflow   41
     Growing in Love

18   What Do You
     Need?   43
     God's Care

19   Three in One   45
     Trinity

20   Hang On!   47
     Growing

21   Master Computer   49
     Mind of Christ

22   Inside Change   51
     Conversion

23   Find Your Roots   53
     Stability

24   Be Prepared   55
     Being Equipped

25   Keep in Step   57
     Teamwork

26 Put to the Test   59
   Testing

27 Come to My
   House   61
   Indwelling Spirit

28 It's a Mystery   63
   Mystery

29 Be Careful   65
   The Tongue

30 Let's Be Partners   67
   Cooperation

31 Can I Help?   69
   Authority

32 Open Up   71
   Openmindedness

33 Tune In   73
   Good News

34 Wonderful!
   Wonderful!   75
   God's Creation

35 Grow Up   77
   Growth

36 Symbol of Love   79
   Symbols

37 Always the Same   81
   Reliability

38 A Proclamation   83
   Proclaiming Christ

39 Be Comfortable   85
   Gift of Peace

40 Wonders of the
   World   87
   Joy

41 Hit the Target   89
   Ultimate Goal

42 Turn Over   91
   Submission

43 Solid as a Rock   93
   Steadfastness

44 Who Cares?   95
   Special Care

45 The Right
   Direction   97
   Guidance

46 Strength of a
   Horse   99
   Strength

47 Two Peas in a
   Pod   101
   Equality

48 Purr-fect Peace   103
   Contentment

49 Touch the Skies   105
   Greatness

50 Respectfully
   Yours   107
   Respect

Preface

H ave you ever struggled to prepare a Bible lesson that will interest lively children? Often the moment children think they are going to be "taught" they become withdrawn, fidgety, or downright hostile. Some tend to view education as a painful event.

Over the years as I raised two sons and was involved with children in school projects, organizations, sports activities, Sunday school, junior church, and Vacation Bible School, I came to appreciate how unique and special children are. By their very nature they are energetic, curious, creative, honest, and open to new ideas. They notice and find joy in ordinary objects around them. By tapping into this reservoir of natural enthusiasm with an idea or theme with which they can readily identify, I have found that their excitement is visible. Christianity is an exciting personal experience and it can be presented to children in that same spirit.

The fifty biblical lessons in this book are offered in a positive way that emphasizes not only the sound principles of the Bible but also an appreciation of our everyday world.

During the past eighteen months, the lessons in this book have been used by a pastor and an elementary school teacher who are especially interested in children. To test the effectiveness and the ease with which the concepts could be presented, they used the ideas during the morning worship service as "A Time with Children." Judging by the expressions of anticipation on the faces of the children and their willingness to respond and be involved in the lessons, the material has been a success.

A surprising spin-off has been the enthusiasm and interest with which the adults in the congregation responded. They liked the simple, concise way the concepts were illustrated and enjoyed the expressions on the faces of the children and their ad-lib comments. The time devoted to the children's lesson has become a favorite part of the church's worship service.

The lesson ideas are not classified according to age, type of class, or size of group. Applied as a guide, they can be expanded or edited to meet the needs of a particular situation. The material should be used in a creative way that encourages child participation in the learning process. In addition to asking questions, if a child can see, feel, smell, touch, and perhaps taste in the process of being exposed to an idea, that idea becomes more forceful and real. One concept that is well illustrated can offer unlimited opportunities for growth.

Children represent hope, progress, and the continuation of love in the world. We need their resource of inquisitive, active enthusiasm, and they need our help in understanding the sound principles found in the Bible—principles that are really a prescription for happy, productive lives.

1
Choosing What Is Best

Object: Five sets of paired objects: banana and banana peel; fresh bread and stale, moldy bread; smooth paper and wrinkled paper; a fresh flower and a wilted flower; a long, sharpened pencil and a short, dull one.

Concept: Making good choices.

Text: *Philippians 1:9* (TEV) "I pray that your love will keep on growing more and more, together with true knowledge and perfect judgment, so that you will be able to choose what is best."

L ook at the items before you and *choose what is best* from each set of two. *(They do so.)*

Why did you choose the banana instead of the peel, fresh bread instead of stale, moldy bread, smooth paper instead of wrinkled? Why did you choose a fresh flower and long pencil? The reason you chose the items you did is because they are more useful or beautiful. No one wants to eat a banana peel or moldy bread. Who would write on wrinkled paper if smooth paper was available? Everyone enjoys a fresh flower more than a wilted one. And a long pencil will last longer than a short one.

When you looked at the sets of items and decided which one was best, you were making a choice. The decision was simple because it was easy to see which item was more valuable and beneficial.

Not all choices are this simple. Every day it is necessary to make decisions. Often it is difficult to decide what is best. Perhaps the choice is between two things, both of which seem good. Perhaps we must say no because all options are negative in some way. Sometimes we forget that we have the ability to make choices.

The Bible offers advice about making good choices. The apostle Paul said, "I pray that your love will keep on growing more and more, together with true knowledge and perfect judgment, so that you will be able to choose what is best."

The key to making good choices seems to be that we continue to grow in love. As we learn more about God and receive his love, we become more loving individuals. We are more concerned about others and about making good choices for ourselves as well.

God has true knowledge and perfect judgment and as we study his ways we can strive to become more like him. As we grow in the knowledge of God we will be given the ability to *choose what is best.*

2
Behind and Ahead

Object: Soap bubbles. A picture of a rainbow. Crystal prism or a piece of crystal jewelry. A flashlight (use this to reflect the colors from a crystal prism onto white paper).

Concept: Putting sin behind us and Christ ahead of us.

Text: *Genesis 9:13* "I have set my rainbow in the clouds, and it will be the sign of the covenant between me and the earth."

W hat color is sunshine? We usually think of it as being yellow or white, but would it surprise you to know that there are many colors in sunlight?

If conditions are just right and you know what to look for, you will be able to see that sunlight can be red, orange, yellow, green, blue, and violet.

There are two words we need to understand before we look for the different colors in sunshine. One is *prism* and the other is *spectrum*. A prism is an object that breaks up light and forms it into a band of colors. The band of colors is called a spectrum.

A crystal prism will help us see how that happens. The prism is transparent and so when it's twirled, look what happens. *(Twirl prism.)* It catches the light and throws it outward. You can see different colors in the prism even though the crystal is clear.

Now let's blow some soap bubbles. *(Blow bubbles.)* If you look closely, you will see that they are breaking the light into many colors.

Two things must happen before we can see all the colors in sunshine. Rain must be falling and the sun must be shining at the same time. As sunlight travels through the raindrops a spectrum is formed. If we look straight ahead *(point forward)* toward the rain with the sun shining behind us *(point behind)* we will be able to see a rainbow. When you look at a rainbow you are seeing all the colors in sunshine. A rainbow is one of God's most lovely gifts to us.

Just as two things must happen before we can see a rainbow, two things are necessary if we are to receive an even greater gift from God. The Bible instructs us to put sin behind us *(point behind)* by asking for forgiveness for the mistakes we have made. We are then encouraged to look ahead *(point forward)* and accept God's love through Jesus Christ. By doing this we will receive God's greatest gift—eternal life.

Just as God promised to send a rainbow, he also promised us his eternal love.

3
The Other Side

Object: Picture of a ferryboat or a large body of water.

Concept: God's faithfulness in leading us through life and, finally, to heaven.

Text: *Genesis 28:15* "I will not leave you until I have done what I have promised you."

A ferryboat is used to transport people, vehicles, and goods across a body of water. Double-ended ferries allow people to drive or walk onto one end of the ferry and exit from the opposite end when the boat reaches the other side. A ferry is a connection between two points.

A ferryboat ride can be an exciting journey. It is fun to watch the waves and feel the boat glide over the water. Often there are beautiful sights to enjoy.

When one buys a ticket to ride on a ferry, the captain and crew assume the responsibility to take the passengers to the other side of the river or bay. They aren't abandoned halfway across. Ferry personnel have been trained to see that passengers safely reach their destination.

In the Old Testament, God told his people, "I will not leave you until I have done what I have promised you." He led them out of Egypt and into the Promised Land. The people felt his presence with them during the journey. He didn't take them part of the way and then abandon them. He stayed with them and remained true to his promise.

The words from the Old Testament are useful to us today. God has promised us eternal life through Jesus Christ. Christ is our connection with God. He has taken the responsibility for our past mistakes and offered forgiveness. If we have faith and believe in his power, we are assured of his presence. His Spirit becomes part of us and guides us toward our destination. The Christian life can be an exciting journey. We can expect God to be true to his promise. "I will not leave you until I have done what I have promised you."

4
Living Power

Object: A long, thin balloon. Picture of a rocket, during launch if possible.

Concept: God's great power at work in our lives.

Text: *Ephesians 1:19* (TEV) "... and how very great is his power at work in us who believe."

Have you ever watched a space ship lift off? Then you've seen the tremendous power of the rocket engines. Considering its size, the rocket is the most powerful type of engine. It can travel faster than any other vehicle. Have you ever thought about how all that power is created?

The rocket burns a mixture of fuel inside the engine with explosive force. When the fuel burns it turns into a gas, causing pressure to build up and push out in all directions. Because the rocket is open at one end, the burning gases escape and the pressure inside pushes the rocket in the opposite direction.

We can use a balloon to demonstrate how a rocket works. When we blow into a balloon we fill it with gas. *(Inflate balloon.)* Now watch the gas escape and the pressure inside push the balloon through the air. *(Let the balloon go.)* That push is called thrust.

Another word that is linked with rockets is payload. The payload is what the rocket carries. Rockets transport scientific instruments for space exploration and research. They also carry astronauts, as we all know. The instruments and men are the payload.

It is exciting to think about the power of rockets. It is also thrilling to know that there is a source of power available to *us*. A verse in the Bible states, ". . . and how very great is his power at work in us who believe." Our faith is the key to that power. As we learn more about God, we will discover the power of his message.

The power of God's love will give a thrust to our lives and get us started in the right direction. If we carry love as our payload we will use God's love in the best way and see powerful results.

Let God be the powerful force in your life.

5
Unlimited Possibilities

Object: Picture of a hummingbird. Pea to illustrate size of a hummingbird egg. Stick of gum to demonstrate the weight of a hummingbird.

Concept: God is able to help us overcome difficulties on our way to discovering our abilities and talents.

Text: *Philippians 4:13* (TEV) "I have the strength to face all conditions by the power that Christ gives me."

H ave you ever heard of a bird that can't sing or walk? There is such a bird and when it is hatched from its pea-sized egg, this bird is an ugly blackish color and is naked and blind.

The bird I'm talking about is the ruby-throated hummingbird. As an adult it's three to four inches long from the tip of its tail to the end of its beak. It weighs less than a stick of gum. The adult male is a dazzle of brilliant color; the female is less colorful.

The hummingbird can fly in ways no other bird can. It flies not only forward, but backward as well. It can fly straight up, zigzag sideways, or stay in the same place by hovering like a helicopter. The hummingbird has powerful wings that beat sixty to seventy times every second. It can fly at speeds up to fifty miles per hour.

When hummingbirds migrate to their winter home they fly five hundred miles without stopping for food or rest.

The hummingbird has a long, thin bill and a tongue like a tube that reaches into a flower and pumps out nectar. Because they use so much energy they need to refuel often and eat hundreds of times a day.

So, the hummingbird that began life quite ugly and helpless has developed into one of the most beautiful and powerful of God's creations.

We are all created by God and each of us has special abilities and talents. The handicaps we have can be overcome if we are willing to explore the possibilities God has for us.

A verse in the New Testament tells us that we have the "strength to face all conditions by the power that Christ gives." We are encouraged to use our unique talents and capabilities to glorify God. Through Christ we are able to find God's purpose for our lives and are given the strength and power to do what God asks of us.

When we search for God's plan for our lives and use the talents he has given us, we experience his power and add beauty to the world. We become one of God's most beautiful and wondrous creations.

6

New Discoveries

Object: A magnifying glass and interesting objects to examine.

Concept: Bible study and prayer help us make new discoveries about who God is.

Text: *Ephesians 1:17* "I keep asking that the God of our Lord Jesus Christ, the glorious Father, may give you the Spirit of wisdom and revelation, so that you may know him better."

About three hundred years ago the microscopic lens was invented. Before that time, there were many things in the world that people didn't know about because they couldn't see them. Almost half the plants in the world can't be seen by the human eye without the aid of a magnifying glass. Also, thousands of small forms of animal life are unseen unless some sort of magnifying instrument is used. By using a hand lens or microscope, we are able to study and enjoy objects that are otherwise invisible.

A magnifying lens is a curved piece of glass that is thicker in the center than at the edges. Because of the thick center and thin edge, the light rays are slowed down and bent toward the center, causing the object to appear larger. The lens allows us to see more clearly and better understand what it is we are studying. It can show us beautiful and unusual shapes in common objects. *(Demonstrate.)*

If you have a magnifying glass at home, you can use it to examine water from a pond or a mud puddle, sugar or salt crystals, a feather, paper, insects, a leaf, newspaper print, or a strand of hair. Anything that is magnified is likely to surprise you in some way. You will make many exciting discoveries with your magnifying glass. You will have something revealed to you that you didn't know before. These discoveries are called revelations.

A revelation, when used in the Bible, means almost the same thing. It is a discovery that reveals God to us.

There are many things that we don't understand about God. Because we can't see him with our eyes we have many questions. By studying the Bible, just as we study objects under a magnifying lens, we can learn more about God. Through prayer his love is revealed to us. Bible study and prayer allow us to see more clearly and understand who God is.

God's love can add beauty to our lives, just as a magnifying glass shows us beauty in ordinary things.

If you choose to find out more about God, your life can be a wonderful adventure full of new discoveries!

7

Button Up

Object: Assortment of buttons. (Use buttons on the children's clothing to further illustrate the idea.)

Concept: Living in union with God and others.

Text: *Philippians 3:1* (TEV) "... be joyful in your union with the Lord."

H ow many in our group have buttons on their clothing? Many of us do.

Buttons come in many shapes, sizes, and colors. They can be made from plastic, metal, wood, leather, glass, shells, or pearls. Some are hand-painted and others are carved from ivory.

Long ago buttons were set with jewels and used as a decoration and a sign of wealth. Later, when people began to wear fitted clothes, buttons were used to hold parts of the garments together. Now, billions of buttons are made each year and they are both beautiful and practical.

What is the purpose of a button? It brings two parts of a garment together. When the button is pushed through a buttonhole, the opening of the garment is fastened together.

When we talk about the purpose of buttons, we could say that they are used to hold, fasten, join, or attach. We could also say that buttons bring about a *union* by connecting the two pieces of the garment. *Union* means to bring together or unite.

A passage in the Bible tells us to "be joyful in our union with the Lord." We are people who were created by God, and because we receive his love and believe in him we become united with him. We are able to form a "union with the Lord." The verse also instructs us to "be joyful." With God's love within us we have the ability to be thankful for many things—parents, family, friends, food, home, church, and the wonderful miracles of our world and universe.

God's love fastens us to him and makes us feel secure. It brings people together and unites them. We can be joined to him by prayer and receive his love and joy.

The next time you button your blouse or shirt, think about the idea of being in union with the Lord. Think about how you can join with others to further God's work through his love.

8

Sweet as Honey

Object: Container of honey. Honeycomb. Pictures of bees or hives. Baked goods made with honey.

Concept: Like honey, kind words are of great value.

Text: *Proverbs 16:24* (TEV) "Kind words are like honey— sweet to the taste and good for your health."

Honey is a thick, natural sugar made by bees. The bees sip a watery liquid called nectar from flowers and store it in a honey bag inside their body. The nectar is then carried to the hive where it is collected in a wax honeycomb that the bees have built. As water evaporates from the nectar, it becomes thick.

One pound of honey is made from nectar collected from over two million flowers! Can you imagine how many trips would be necessary to collect that much nectar?

It's easy to understand why honey is so special. It's used to make candy and baked goods. Breads, pastries, and cookies made with honey stay fresh longer.

Honey is easy to digest because it is a simple sugar. It also can soothe an irritated throat. Many cough syrups and other medicines have honey in them.

People today and centuries ago have valued honey as

one of the most delicious and rarest of foods. In ancient times it was a sign of great riches and wealth.

Honey is mentioned several times in the Bible. Proverbs 16:24 is a good example. "Kind words are like honey—sweet to the taste and good for your health."

A kind word may be as simple as a friendly hello. It may be a sincere thank you to someone who has been helpful. Kind words can also be used to help people who may be lonely or discouraged. Words used in a considerate way are highly valued by others. Kind words are the mark of a rich life.

When we speak in a gentle, loving way our words can bring joy to others. Kind words make people feel better—like honey they are "sweet and good for your health!"

9
Under Cover

Object: Transparent tape. Masking tape. Adhesive tape.

Concept: Like tape, use love to fix things.

Text: *1 Peter 4:8* (TEV) "Above everything, love one another earnestly, because love covers over many sins."

T here are three kinds of tape that can be found in most homes. Transparent tape is used to repair a tear on a piece of paper. It brings the edges together, covers the tear, and makes the page strong again. Transparent tape is also useful for art and craft projects.

Masking tape is another type of tape that can be used to mend tears and hold things together. Sometimes people put masking tape around the edges of an object they are painting to keep paint from splattering onto other areas.

Adhesive tape is used to hold a bandage over a sore or a wound. It covers the bandage and keeps it dry.

Each of these three types of tape are used to bring things together, to repair and cover a damaged area.

The Bible gives us some advice on how to repair mistakes we have made. "Above everything, love one another earnestly, because love covers over many sins."

The mistakes that we and others make are called sins. Sin makes us feel bad and can hurt other people. We all make mistakes. No person is perfect. We sometimes say or do hurtful things.

Sometimes our family or friends do things that bother us. They may hurt us by their actions and the words they use.

We all have things to work on and correct in our lives. When we love God we can ask for forgiveness for the mistakes we have made and be free to love others. When we try to love others we can forgive them for hurting us and learn to be a better friend. Because of God's love, he forgives us and we can use that love to forgive others. Love is the most important resource we have. Love covers the damage, brings people together, and makes them strong.

Tape is used to repair and cover a damaged area and to join things together. Love can be used in the same way. Test it. Try it and see the results. Love fixes things.

10
Sing a Song

Object: A comb (to demonstrate how grasshoppers and crickets produce sound). A live cricket or grasshopper in a jar, if possible (otherwise, a picture of one or both will do).

Concept: By using our voices in song, we are able to give God thanks.

Text: *Ephesians 5:19* "Speak to one another with psalms, hymns and spiritual songs. Sing and make music in your heart to the Lord, always giving thanks to God the Father for everything, in the name of our Lord Jesus Christ."

There are insects in our world that make music in unusual ways. Two examples are the cricket and the grasshopper. A grasshopper has long hind legs with a row of tiny pegs on the upper, inner portion of each leg. When these pegs are rubbed against the hard edge of one of the grasshopper's wings, a musical sound is produced. Some grasshoppers rub their hind legs together to make music.

A cricket has ridges and also a sharp-edged area on its wings. When the wings are rubbed together, the cricket is said to be "singing."

Only male crickets and grasshoppers sing and they

do so to attract a female. The music may sound like a chirp, crackle, click, or creak. It may be soft or loud. The grasshopper tends to sing during the heat of a summer day and the cricket in the evening when it is cooler.

If we run our fingers over the teeth of a comb, we can begin to understand how insect music is produced. *(Demonstrate this.)*

Another unusual thing about a cricket is that its ears are on its front legs. A grasshopper has ears on its abdomen. We could say that these insects make music and hear music in an extraordinary way!

In the Bible there is a verse that instructs us to "speak to one another with psalms, hymns, and spiritual songs." The verse continues, "Sing and make music in your heart to the Lord, always giving thanks to God the Father for everything, in the name of our Lord Jesus Christ."

God has given us many wonderful things. Our world is full of beauty and the miracles of his creation. God's greatest gift to us is his constant love. This love was demonstrated for us in the life of Jesus Christ.

One way we can thank God and share our joy with others is through music. Like the legs and wings of the grasshopper and cricket, our voices are musical instruments and can be used to worship God. During a church service we have an opportunity to sing hymns together. You may want to sing in the choir or perform solos for others to enjoy. Whether you are singing or listening, music can be fun. Use your voice and your ears to appreciate music and give thanks to God.

11
Are You Positive?

Object: Pencil.

Concept: Living in a positive manner.

Text: *Ecclesiastes 7:20* (TEV) "There is no one on earth who does what is right all the time and never makes a mistake."

A pencil is something you use in school every day. Pencils are so much a part of our lives that we don't really think about them.

People have had pencils, similar to those we use today, for about three hundred years. The inside of a pencil is made of a substance called graphite. This graphite, which comes from the earth, is mixed with clay and pressed into a long, thin shape, then put into ovens to bake. The graphite mixture is then placed into grooves that have been cut in a piece of cedar. This is the bottom half of the pencil. The other half is then glued on top. Finally, the pencils are shaped, sanded, varnished, and stamped with information.

One interesting thing about a pencil is that each end has an opposite function. We use one end to write or draw. We use it to make lists, do arithmetic problems, write stories, create beautiful pictures, or copy directions. It is useful!

At the opposite end of the pencil is an eraser, which we use when we want to remove what the other part of the pencil has done. The eraser can't be used to draw pictures or write stories. Its purpose is to remove mistakes.

When we go to school or work we should try to make our lives like the tip of the pencil—useful, creative, and helpful. Just as we must use the pencil to get results, we must use our abilities to get results.

Don't let your life become like an eraser. An eraser is more negative than positive. Its sole purpose is to try to remove mistakes. We need to encourage others in a positive way, not look for their flaws.

Sometimes we make mistakes that are sins. In the Bible it says that "there is not a single man in all the earth who is always good and never sins."

We all sin and we need to remember that if we talk about our mistakes with God, he will forgive us. God can erase the negative things that we do and give us a new start.

Choose to live your life in a positive, useful way, like the writing end of the pencil. Let God take care of the mistakes and erase the sins.

12
Listen Carefully

Object: Diagram showing interior of ear. Pictures of things people hear.

Concept: We should make good use of our ears to hear God's Word.

Text: *Hebrews 2:1* "We must pay more careful attention, therefore, to what we have heard, so that we do not drift away."

Your ears are one of the most remarkable parts of your body. Because of them, you are able to hear rain falling, traffic noises, wind in the trees, bells, laughter, voices talking, and many kinds of music.

Sound waves enter through a canal in the *outer* ear *(point to someone's ear)* and hit against the *eardrum* which is stretched tightly between the outer and *middle* parts of the ear *(point to this and the following on diagram)*. The eardrum vibrates when the sound waves hit it and these vibrations are transferred to three tiny bones located in the middle ear. These bones are called the hammer, anvil, and stirrup. The stirrup sends the vibrations through an opening into the inner part of the ear. The inner ear is filled with fluid and the sound waves pass through the fluid and move tiny hairs that line the bony loops of the inner ear. From these hairs in the inner ear the vibration is picked up by nerve fibers and sent to the brain.

As you can see, our sense of hearing, which we sometimes take for granted, is a complicated but wonderful function of our body.

The Bible advises us to use our ears in an active way. "We must pay more careful attention, therefore, to what we have heard, so that we do not drift away." To listen we must pay attention or "tune in." Many sounds and noises are all around us, but to notice and make use of those sounds we must pay attention.

We have many opportunities to hear what God has to say to us. We can hear God's Word from the pastor's sermon, choir music, Sunday school class, Bible readings, the radio, or even from a friend. To understand the truth of what we are hearing we must listen carefully. When we make good use of our ears we learn and grow and can appreciate more of what God has intended for us.

13
Threefold

Object: Glass of water, ice cubes. Picture of a steaming teapot or a steaming cup of coffee if available.

Concept: The three forms of water illustrate the Trinity.

Text: *2 Corinthians 13:14* "May the grace of the Lord Jesus Christ, and the love of God, and the fellowship of the Holy Spirit be with you all."

We are all familiar with water. We drink it, bathe in it, cook with it, and use it to wash our clothes. In fact, water is necessary for life. It accounts for two-thirds of our body weight. Seventy percent of the surface of the earth is covered with water!

In the kitchen we can find water in three forms. Water runs out of the kitchen faucet in the liquid form. When water is exposed to below freezing temperatures it develops crystals and becomes solid. The solid form of water can be found in the freezer trays of the refrigerator. We call it ice. When water is heated to a high temperature, it turns into a vapor, or gas, called steam. Steam can be felt or seen over a boiling pot of water on the stove.

In nature we can also see the three forms of water. Rain is the liquid form. Ice on a pond is the solid form.

Clouds, fog, or steamy vapor rising from the ground is water in the form of a gas.

God is described in the Bible as having three forms, too. The three forms of God—or the three *persons* of God—are called the Trinity. This is a difficult thing to understand, but just as water is the same thing in three unique forms, so is God the same thing in three unique forms. All three parts of God are One but they have different functions. Because of his love, God the Father created us and the universe. God the Son came to earth in the form of a man, Jesus Christ, to demonstrate God's love and bring salvation. The Holy Spirit is a form of God who is sent to bring us understanding, joy, and comfort. God works in a person's life in all three forms. Through faith we believe in one God who has three forms, three persons. "May the grace of the Lord Jesus Christ, and the love of God, and the fellowship of the Holy Spirit be with you all."

14
Something Extra

Object: A box of Cracker Jacks.

Concept: Open the Bible to find the "prize" of eternal life.

Text: *Romans 6:23* (TEV) "... God's free gift is eternal life in union with Christ Jesus our Lord.

I would like to share a box of Cracker Jacks with you. We can all enjoy a sample. *(Distribute.)*

There is something extra in a box of Cracker Jacks and it is usually found at the bottom of the box after all the peanuts and popcorn have been eaten: a free gift. It's fun to see what the prize will be. It could be a puzzle, a small toy, a ring, a tiny book, or a picture. The problem with these small toys is that they are easily broken or lost. Also, because there is only one gift in the box, most of us will not get one.

The Bible tells us that God has a free gift for us that lasts forever. Just as you must open the box of Cracker Jacks to find the prize, you must open the Bible to find out about God's free gift. "God's free gift is eternal life in union with Christ Jesus our Lord."

If we believe in Jesus Christ as our Lord we are given life that never ends. The gift of eternal life is the best prize of all because it is always available to us and it is for everyone. We don't need to dig to the bottom of a box to find the gift, we just need to ask for it.

After we have received God's "prize," it is ours forever. It can't be lost or broken. It is given to us because of God's love for us.

Enjoy God's free gift. It is yours forever!

15

One of a Kind

Object: Picture of a penguin. Ice cubes. If available, freeze snowballs during the winter and keep in the freezer for an unusual summer presentation.

Concept: Using our uniqueness to glorify God.

Text: *Genesis 1:31* "God saw all that he had made, and it was very good."

The penguin is a bird far different from the birds we see flying in the sky. It cannot fly, except underwater where it puts its flipper-like wings and webbed feet to good use. The penguin stands upright, like a person. Because it has short legs it takes small steps and walks with a comical waddle. Because penguins are awkward on land, they sometimes travel by sliding over the ice on their stomachs. This bird even sleeps while it is standing.

Although there are many things about penguins that to us seem strange and amusing, they are exceptional birds, well suited for their life in those regions of the world where the temperature may be as cold as forty to one hundred degrees below zero.

Their black and white feathers are short, dense, and waterproof. They also have a thick layer of fat on their bodies to keep them warm. The penguin is an excellent swimmer and diver. They can swim for great distances nd reach speeds of up to thirty miles per hour. They can dive far down into the water and leap above the surface in a graceful arc.

The emperor penguin is the largest kind of penguin and can grow to be four feet tall, weighing almost one hundred pounds. An interesting thing about emperor penguins is that after the mother lays an egg, the father rolls it on top of his feet and tucks his fat body over it to keep it warm. He cares for the egg in this way for sixty-four days. He doesn't eat at all during those two months and may lose half of his body weight. After the egg is hatched the mother returns from the sea with food. She then cares for the baby penguin while the male goes to the sea to find food.

The penguin, like everything else in our universe, was created by God. Genesis 1:31 tells us that "God saw all that he had made and it was very good."

The penguin is an unusual bird but it is an excellent creation. No other bird possesses its special qualities. Although in some ways the black and white birds may seem awkward and comical, they are beautiful and graceful as they glide, float, dive, and turn in the water. They glorify God in their unique way.

God also created you! He "saw all that he had made and it was very good."

You are special. There is no one else in the whole world exactly like you. You have talents and skills that are uniquely your own. Each one of us must discover our special talents and skills and use them to add beauty to the world.

By being ourselves, we fit into God's plan. Be like the penguin and use your unusual and unique abilities to glorify God.

16
A Good Flavor

Object: A bowl of water. Salt. Pepper. Liquid dishwashing detergent.

Concept: God's love chases away our sins and helps us to love others.

Text: *Mark 9:50* (TEV) "Salt is good; but if it loses its saltiness, how can you make it salty again? Have the salt of friendship among yourselves, and live in peace with one another."

The Bible teaches us that Christians are like salt. Christian love flavors the world, just as salt flavors food. Not only does salt make food taste better, but it is necessary for people to have it in their diets if they want to stay healthy.

Love not only makes the world a better place to live, but like salt, love is necessary for everyone. We could not live without love. We all need to know that someone cares about us and we need to love others, too. We can never give or have too much love. The more love we have, the more we have to give to others.

There is one thing that gets in the way of love. Do you know what that is? Sin. When we have sin in our lives we aren't free to give or receive love.

Let me show you what I mean. Let's pretend that the

water in this bowl is your life and that this salt is love. I'll shake some "love" into your "life." It goes into your "life" so easily. The "life" seems to absorb all of the "love." We know it is there, even though we can't see it, because it gives flavor. If you tasted the water it would taste salty. When people have love in their lives, their lives have flavor—a better taste.

Now, pretend that this pepper is sin. I'm going to shake some "sin" into this "life" of yours. Here go some little lies. Some unkind words. Some greediness. What else? Disobedience?

Notice what is happening. The "life" is getting messy. The "sin" is covering the "love." We can see the "sin" and it is ugly.

There is a solution for this problem. The perfect source of love is God. He loves unconditionally—a large word that means he loves us just the way we are. Even if our lives are ugly with sin, God loves us! And because God's love is perfect and powerful, it is able to chase the sin away and uncover the love that is in all of us.

Pretend that this detergent is God's love. All we need is a tiny drop and as we add it to the bowl of water, notice what happens. *(Add a drop of detergent to water.)*

God's love can work in your life just that fast. He is always ready to forgive us for our sins and chase them away. When we ask him to do that, he uncovers our love.

The people of the world need love, just as food needs salt. "Have the salt of friendship among yourselves, and live in peace with one another."

Suggestion: Experiment before presenting this lesson.

17
Grow and Overflow

Object: Loaf of bread. Package of yeast. Optional: warm water, sugar, loaf of warm bread.

Concept: God's Word will help God's love within us to grow.

Text: *1 Thessalonians 3:12* "May the Lord make your love increase and overflow for each other and for everyone else, just as ours does for you."

Have you ever had a chance to smell bread baking at home or in a bakery? The fragrance of freshly-baked bread is a great joy and a special treat.

This loaf of fresh bread is golden brown on the outside, and *(cut loaf in half)* soft and white on the inside. It has a wonderful aroma and a delicious taste!

When bread is made, there is one important ingredient that must be added—yeast. Yeast is what makes the bread rise and become soft and light.

Yeast is actually a one-celled plant that cannot be seen without a microscope. It grows by sending out little buds and branches. When sugar—a source of food for the yeast cells—is added to the bread dough, carbon dioxide is given off and bubbles are formed inside the loaf of bread. Heat causes the gas to expand and so the bread rises. If the bread dough is left sitting too long without being checked, the yeast will continue to work and the dough will keep rising, and eventually it will overflow the bowl.

God's love works the same way. If we feed the love within us with God's Word, the love keeps expanding. We can't keep it inside. It grows until it overflows to others.

Each of you has the capacity to grow and become more loving. Let your love overflow to others and you will feel joy.

Suggestion: If time and situation permit, add warm water and sugar to the yeast and watch it bubble. For a special treat, share a loaf of warm bread with the children.

18
What Do You Need?

Object: A picture of a kangaroo. A soft, warm, pouch-like bag.

Concept: We can depend upon God to meet our needs and help us grow.

Text: *Matthew 6:8* (TEV) "... Your Father already knows what you need before you ask him."

Philippians 4:19 "And my God will meet all your needs according to his glorious riches in Christ Jesus."

Kangaroos are fascinating animals. They are marsupials—a large word that means that the female kangaroo has a pouch.

When a baby kangaroo is born it is about an inch long and weighs less than an ounce. It is blind and has no fur to keep it warm. As soon as it is born, the baby kangaroo—called a joey—crawls into the mother's pouch. Once inside, the weak, helpless joey finds milk, warmth, and protection. It stays there for about six months or until it is able to take care of itself. Even when the kangaroo is older it will return to the pouch for food or security.

An adult male kangaroo is called a boomer and can weigh up to two hundred pounds. The female, called a flyer, is smaller but can run faster. Kangaroos have large, powerful back legs and feet and can jump twenty-five feet in one leap. They are timid animals but they can be fierce fighters if they need to defend themselves.

The Bible has a verse that describes how God takes care of us, just as a mother kangaroo takes care of her joey. "Your Father already knows what you need before you ask him."

A mother kangaroo knows exactly what her baby needs, and because she gives the joey milk, warmth, and closeness, it grows strong.

When we feel weak and helpless and we need to be close to someone, that someone can be God.

Another verse in the Bible says, "And my God will meet all your needs according to his glorious riches in Christ Jesus."

The mother kangaroo gives her baby life by carrying it in her pouch. When a joey is in the pouch all its needs are met and it feels safe and secure.

God has given us eternal life through his Son, Jesus Christ. When we depend on that promise we also can feel safe and secure.

The most important thing to learn from our talk about kangaroos is that we can depend on God just as the joey depends on its mother. By staying close to her, the joeys develop into enormous, powerful animals; by staying close to God, we can develop into strong Christians who are able to be happy and secure in the world.

19
Three in One

Object: An apple. A jar of applesauce. Dried apple slices.

Concept: God is Father, Son, and Holy Spirit.

Text: *Matthew 28:19* "Therefore go and make disciples of all nations, baptizing them in the name of the Father and of the Son and of the Holy Spirit...."

D o you like apples? Look at this beautiful red apple and think about its qualities. An apple is a natural food that grows on a tree. Nothing needs to be added to it and nothing needs to be removed. It seems perfect. I will slice the apple so we can all enjoy its crunchy good taste. *(Slice and distribute.)*

The apples in this jar have been peeled and cooked into applesauce. They are soft instead of crunchy and their flavor is different. They have been changed into another form.

Now let's eat a piece of a dried apple. *(Distribute.)* The pieces feel like leather and are chewy. The color has changed to light brown.

The fresh apple, the applesauce, and the dried apple are all apples but they seem completely different. They look different, their texture is different, and they taste different. What we have is the very same thing in three different forms. But they all have the same purpose: they're good to eat!

Have you ever heard anyone talk about the Trinity? Many adults are confused about that subject. In church we talk about the three forms of the Trinity as the Father, Son, and Holy Spirit. How can three different things be the same? Think about the Trinity in the way we thought about the apple—the very same thing in three different forms. God created the heavens and the earth. Jesus Christ, God's Son, came to earth in the form of man to bring salvation. The Holy Spirit comes into our lives to guide and comfort us. All three are God in three different forms. They all have the same purpose: they want us to experience God's love!

Suggestions: This lesson could be expanded by making applesauce.

20

Hang On!

Object: Fresh, canned, frozen, or dried beans. A seed packet of beans with a picture of garden beans on the front.

Concept: We can learn from the bean plant about what it takes to grow into strong, valuable Christians.

Text: *Hebrews 4:14* (TEV) "Let us, then, hold firmly to the faith we profess. For we have a great High Priest who has gone into the very presence of God—Jesus, the Son of God."

 $\mathbf{B}$ eans are one of our most valuable foods because they contain so many things that are good for our bodies. They taste good, too!

Some beans are dried and are used to make chili or bean casseroles. Green beans are picked while the seeds are still in the pod and may be eaten when they are raw or after they have been cooked, canned, or frozen.

Beans are not only good for us, but they are also good for the earth because they add nitrogen to the soil in which they grow.

Bean plants grow like vines, wrapping themselves around a pole or string—whatever is put there to support them. The bean plant will cling to that support; without it, the plant would grow in all directions and form a tangled mess. Another interesting fact about bean plants is that they seem to grow in the direction of the sun as it passes over in the sky.

We can learn about ourselves and God by thinking about how beans grow. They hold firmly to support and grow toward the sun.

The Bible tells us to hold firmly to our faith in Christ. He is our support and light. From him we get our strength and direction. Without direction and support our lives can get tangled into a mess.

If we direct our lives toward Jesus we will grow to be strong, valuable Christians.

Let God give support and direction to your life. Cling tightly to the promise he has given us for a good life now and forevermore.

21

Master Computer

Object: A pocket calculator. Pictures of computers if available.

Concept: The human brain is a marvelous thing; as Christians we have the mind of Christ.

Text: *1 Corinthians 2:16* "But we have the mind of Christ."

Computers have become an important part of our lives. We see them when we go to the grocery store, in office buildings, at school, and even in our homes. When we push the right buttons a computer will add, subtract, multiply, and divide rapidly. They can be used to solve complex problems and can store information for future use. A small computer can help us with our mathematics, homework, while others can make calculations that are so accurate they can be used to send men into space. These big computers can make as many as three million calculations in a second!

Did you know that you yourselves have the most amazing "computer" of all? You have it with you all the time. It is the "master control center" that lies inside your head, called the brain.

No one knows exactly how the human brain works, but we know what it does. Like a telephone switchboard, your brain receives, processes, and sends information to all parts of your body. Everything that you see, hear, taste, feel, touch, or smell is analyzed by the brain. The brain sends out messages to regulate all the body functions and actions. It controls your speech, hunger, thirst, tears, memory, muscles, and the beating of our heart. All of your emotions—your feelings of love, hate, anger, and fear—originate in your brain. The brain also stores all this information for future use. Your brain truly is a marvelous wonder.

God created you and gave you this "master computer" for a reason. We have the ability to think, feel, and remember far beyond our imagination. As Christians we are told in the Bible that although it seems like a mystery, we actually have a part of Christ's mind within us.

Through God's Spirit we are given insight and a better understanding of God's purpose for us. God gives us the wisdom to choose what is best. Use your master computer to learn and grow!

22

Inside Change

Object: An ear of corn. Canned corn. Popcorn in both forms.

Concept: Faith in Christ changes us into something new.

Text: *2 Corinthians 5:17* "Therefore, if anyone is in Christ, he is a new creation; the old has gone, the new has come!"

H ave you seen corn growing in a field or garden? Have you ever bought corn at the supermarket? Corn is very important to our country; it is the biggest farm crop in the United States. The Indians were cultivating and using corn before Columbus came to America.

Can you think of ways we use corn? I'll peel back the husk so you can see the yellow kernels. The most important use of corn is as food, not only for ourselves, but also for livestock.

Can you think of ways that corn is used as a food? Fresh corn on the cob, canned corn, frozen corn. Cereals, sugar, syrup, cornmeal, cornstarch, corn oil—these are also made from corn.

Cornstarch is used in baked goods, baby powder, medicines, and glue. Paints and soaps are manufactured in a process that uses corn oil.

When the kernels have been removed, the portion that

is left is the cob and it, too, has many uses. Cobs are used for fuel and in the manufacturing of nylon and plastics. They are crushed and fed to livestock. Cobs are also ground up into a substance that is used to clean oil from airplane and car engines.

There's another kind of corn besides the one we've been talking about. Do you know what it is? It's popcorn. Feel how hard the kernels are. *(Give them a chance to touch the kernels.)* How do kernels as hard as popcorn become the fluffy white morsels we eat?

When popcorn is heated, the moisture inside turns to steam and the kernel explodes. A similar thing happens to a person who accepts God's love. When people realize that a loving God cares for them and has a plan for their lives, something almost like an explosion takes place within them. As they experience love, joy, and peace, a change takes place in their lives and it shows, just like the popcorn. Because of God's love, they care about others and share their happiness. The fluffy white kernels are still popcorn, but they don't look at all like these hard kernels. Someone who has experienced God's love can be changed into a more beautiful and useful person.

Suggestion: Popcorn or popcorn balls that can be eaten would be a special treat if time and situation permit.

23
Find Your Roots

Object: A plant root.

Concept: We need to be rooted deeply in God's love.

Text: *Ephesians 3:17-18* (TEV) "... I pray that you may have your roots and foundation in love, so that you, together with all God's people, may have the power to understand how broad and long, how high and deep, is Christ's love."

This dirty, twisted object is a root. It is the unseen part of a plant and is very important to our world.

Every plant or tree must have an underground part to anchor it in the soil and keep it steady when the wind blows. As the root grows it pushes downward into the soil, giving the tree more stability and strength. The root also keeps the tree alive by sending food and water upward to the trunk and branches. This nourishment helps the tree produce leaves, flowers, or fruit.

People are in some ways similar to trees. They need to have food and water. They also need something to keep them steady and help them to grow in the best possible way.

Let's think about becoming rooted in God's love. He gives us spiritual food when we look to him through prayer and read the Bible. As we pray and study, we grow and become stronger. We develop a deep root that will hold us upright and keep us steady when problems arise. If we become firmly rooted in God's love, our lives will become as beautiful as the flowers and fruits that form on a tree. We will be useful to others.

Our needs will be met by being firmly rooted in God's marvelous love.

Suggestion: If possible, show a sturdy plant and a non-thriving one.

24

Be Prepared

Object: Backpacking clothing and equipment.

Concept: Scripture equips and supplies us for living.

Text: *2 Timothy 3:16-17* (TEV) "All Scripture is inspired by God and is useful for teaching the truth, rebuking error, correcting faults, and giving instruction for right living, so that the person who serves God may be fully qualified and equipped to do every kind of good deed."

Have you ever spent the night in a sleeping bag in your back yard? It's fun to be outside in the fresh air and be able to look at the night sky.

Backpackers are people who like to hike into the wilderness to enjoy the beautiful scenery. They carry all the supplies they will need in a pack that they carry on their back.

Experienced backpackers know they must plan and prepare for a trip in advance. They exercise to stay in good physical condition. They learn all they can about how to avoid dangerous situations. They study maps and read books to become familiar with the area.

What kind of special clothing and equipment do backpackers need when they hike in the mountains? Comfortable boots and stockings are important. A pack, sleeping bag, tent, warm jacket, compass, maps, first-aid items, food, and cooking utensils are some of the equipment needed to make the trip enjoyable and safe. Can you think of other things a backpacker must consider? A backpacker should be fully qualified and equipped to travel in the wilderness.

The apostle Paul tells us in the New Testament that "all Scripture is inspired by God and is useful for teaching the truth, rebuking error, correcting faults, and giving instruction for right living, so that the person who serves God may be fully qualified and equipped to do every kind of good deed."

As we study and become familiar with the Bible, we will discover the truth of God's message. His love is offered to everyone through his Son, Jesus Christ. His life was an example for us to follow. His teachings give us instruction for how to live a satisfying life. The Scriptures also help us to recognize our faults and correct errors.

As we grow in the knowledge and love of God, we become strong. Our faith increases. An experienced Christian uses God's love to reach out to others. The Bible, which is inspired by God, helps us to become "fully qualified and equipped to do every kind of good deed."

25

Keep in Step

Object: A musical instrument. A picture of a marching band. Baton.

Concept: Christ is the church's "band leader."

Text: *1 Peter 2:21* "To this you were called, because Christ suffered for you, leaving you an example, that you should follow in his steps."

Parades are exciting and full of color. One of the best parts of a parade is the marching band. The band members march briskly in straight rows, their uniforms pressed and bright. The trumpets blare and the thud of the drums vibrates through the air.

The leader swings the baton to start the music and to keep the band members playing and marching as one unit. A good leader is necessary to inspire the members and encourage them to work toward a common goal.

A first-rate band must practice its music and marching in order to improve. Each member must practice alone so that his or her skills will help strengthen the band. As each person cooperates and works to improve, the entire band performs better.

A band member who gets out of step or plays the wrong notes can create problems for the entire band.

His actions can cause other band members to lose sight of the leader, become discouraged, or make mistakes.

Our church is like a marching band. If we follow the examples Christ gave us when he lived on earth, we have a perfect leader. His teachings inspire us to be better people and they encourage us to work for a common goal.

As each member tries to improve and practices loving and helping others, the entire church performs better.

Sin can cause us to get out of step with God and with others. It can affect the church, causing us to lose sight of our leader, become discouraged, or make mistakes.

The Bible encourages us to follow a good leader. "To this you were called, because Christ suffered for you, leaving you an example, that you should follow in his steps." Teamwork keeps the church members marching together as a first-rate unit.

The Christian life can be as exciting and colorful as a parade!

Suggestion: If the situation permits, use records or tapes to let the children experience the music of a marching band.

26
Put to the Test

Object: Tire gauge; items to be tested.

Concept: Just as we test things physically, we need to test things spiritually as well.

Text: *1 Thessalonians 5:21* (TEV) "Put all things to the test; keep what is good and avoid every kind of evil."

E very day we test things. Can you think of examples? When you take a shower you need to test the temperature of the water to see if it's too hot. When you close the door of your house at night, you may want to test it to see whether or not it is locked. Bike and car tires can be tested to see if they have enough air. *(Display tire gauge.)*

A cook will sample the food he's making in order to test it to see if it has enough flavor. Sometimes the first bite we take is a sort of test to see if the food is too hot or if it needs salt. Food can also be tested by smelling it to see if it has spoiled.

You can probably think of other things that get tested. Why do we test things? When we test something we examine it closely. We look it over thoroughly. We want to know if it is good, or if it does what it is meant to do. We also want to know if the situation or object is in some way harmful.

We use our senses to gather information. We may feel, look, taste, smell, and listen when we put something to the test. We use the information to decide if the object or situation is something we want to be involved with or avoid.

A verse in the Bible encourages us to test things. "Put all things to the test: keep what is good and avoid every kind of evil." To follow this biblical advice we must be alert. We must examine situations closely. We need to find out if what we are testing is harmful or beneficial. When we are alert, use our senses, and gather information we are able to make better decisions. Put it to the test!

27

Come to My House

Object: A shell. A picture of a hermit crab.

Concept: God lives in us.

Text: *Hebrews 3:6* (TEV) "But Christ is faithful as the Son in charge of God's house. We are his house if we keep up our courage and our confidence in what we hope for."

A hermit crab lives by the seashore. This crab is unusual because he borrows an empty shell to use as a house and carries it wherever he goes. Because the hermit crab has a soft body, he needs extra protection. When he finds a shell that is the right size he checks it to see if it's empty and clean, then quickly backs in, hooking himself into it with his back legs.

This unusual creature has two large front claws, similar to those of a lobster. They can be used to seal off the opening of the shell, leaving the crab well protected. The front legs can also be left outside the shell and used for walking.

The crab uses the borrowed shell until he outgrows it; then he must find a larger one.

Another unusual fact about the hermit crab is that he often lives with a sea anemone attached to the top of his shell. He finds one attached to a rock, then pats and pokes it until it moves to the top of his shell and attaches itself there. The hermit crab likes to have the anemone as a companion because it gives him more protection. When it becomes necessary for the crab to move from one house to another he takes the sea anemone with him.

As you can see, the hermit crab is not really a hermit, because he lives with a companion.

As Christians we also live with a companion. The Bible tells us that "Christ is faithful as the Son in charge of God's house. We are his house if we keep up our courage and our confidence in what we hope for."

We are God's house. If we are Christians, he lives in us. That may seem mysterious but according to the Scriptures it is true. If God lives in us we have a responsibility to take good care of our bodies. We need to remind ourselves that our body belongs to God. We should eat well, rest, bathe, exercise, and keep damaging things from harming our body.

You are special because God loves you and lives in you. Take care of God's house!

28

It's a Mystery

Object: A number of children's mystery books.

Concept: There will always be things that we don't understand.

Text: *Ecclesiastes 3:11* (TEV) "He has set the right time for everything. He has given us a desire to know the future but never gives us the satisfaction of fully understanding what he does."

W hat is it about a good mystery book that makes it fun to read? It's exciting and interesting. It's also suspenseful—we don't know what to expect. It's a challenge to try to solve the mystery.

As one reads through a mystery book there are clues along the way. One must be alert to pick out those clues, collect the information, and try to fit it all together. We may learn about the characters and their surroundings as we study the clues, but the answer to the mystery isn't revealed until the last pages of the book.

A verse in the Old Testament points out that God and his ways are also a mystery. "He has set the right time for everything. He has given us a desire to know the future but never gives us the satisfaction of fully understanding what he does."

As we grow and become more aware of our surroundings, we may have many questions about God, ourselves, other people, and the world. There are many things we don't understand. Many things seem like mysteries to us.

It is important that we continue to learn and collect information about God, ourselves, other people, and the world. We must be alert to pick out those clues that will help us understand more about the things we question. But, we shouldn't feel troubled if we can't find all the answers we are looking for. Some things will remain a mystery to us.

The good thing about a mystery is that it can make life interesting and exciting. We can be enthused and fascinated as we search for answers. Our curiosity can become a challenge.

If we understood everything fully, there would be no surprises. Perhaps we would even become bored.

The Old Testament verse tells us that God "has set the right time for everything." God has a plan for our lives and when the time is right, the mystery of God and his ways will be revealed to us. The clues will all fit together and the mystery will be solved!

29

Be Careful

Object: A box of wooden matches.

Concept: Our tongues, like matches, can be helpful or harmful.

Text: *James 3:5* "Likewise the tongue is a small part of the body, but it makes great boasts. Consider what a great forest is set on fire by a small spark."

M atches are one of the most useful things we have in our society today. They are important to us because of their convenience and the things which they allow us to do.

Years ago, a fire was started by rubbing stones—called flints—together until friction produced a tiny spark that could be caught in dry leaves or grass. It took patience and steady work to start a fire.

We are fortunate to have matches to use. They allow us to easily start a bonfire or a fire in the fireplace to keep us warm. They are convenient to use when starting a fire for cooking as well.

Modern matches are easy to use because of the way they are constructed. A tiny slice of wood is treated with a chemical so that it won't burn too easily. Then one end of it is soaked in paraffin, a wax, to help it catch fire.

That end is then dipped in chemicals that burn when heat from friction causes a chemical reaction.

Although matches are important to us because they allow us to start helpful fires, they can be dangerous if not used properly.

If small children play with matches they may hurt themselves or others.

A match that is lit in the wrong place can be dangerous. A tiny spark can cause a house fire or forest fire that can hurt people and animals.

We should appreciate matches and be thankful for them but always be aware of their destructive possibilities.

There is a part of your body that is wonderful and useful but that can be dangerous like a match. It is your tongue!

Our tongues help us to talk, taste, and eat food. If we use our voices in the right way we can sing, pray, praise God, and talk with our friends. When we say things in a friendly or encouraging way we make ourselves and our friends feel good.

Our tongue is used incorrectly when we say things that hurt others. Our tongue can be dangerous if we say things that are not true. Just like a match, much damage can be done by a tongue that is not used properly.

To be able to talk and express yourself is a wonderful gift from God. Use your speech in a happy, careful way. Let the things you say benefit yourself and others.

30

Let's Be Partners

Object: A toothbrush.

Concept: We should help one another.

Text: *2 Corinthians 1:4* (TEV) "He helps us in all our troubles, so that we are able to help others who have all kinds of troubles, using the same help that we ourselves have received from God."

T he Egyptian plover or crocodile bird is a small black and white bird that lives by fresh water streams and swamps. When a crocodile comes out of the swamp to sun itself, the plover hops onto the crocodile's back and feeds on parasites that it finds on the large reptile's skin.

When the crocodile obligingly opens its mouth, the plover walks between the huge jaws and eats leeches from around the crocodile's teeth. The large reptile could easily eat the tiny bird but does not.

These two unlikely companions help each other. The crocodile gets clean teeth and the plover gets a meal. This strange relationship between two such different animals is called *symbiosis*. Being together is beneficial to both partners. They live together peacefully.

God helps us in many ways. He understands us, comforts us, and encourages us to become strong individuals. One of the reasons for being healthy, happy, and strong is so that we can help others.

When we find ways to be helpful, we feel better. Helping each other is beneficial to both partners. Cooperation between individuals makes our world seem more friendly and peaceful.

Symbiosis is a good word to remember. It means cooperation, living together peacefully, helping one another.

Let the cooperation between the crocodile and the plover be a reminder of our obligation to the people around us. Use God's wonderful love to reach out to others in a helpful way.

31

Can I Help?

Object: A policeman's badge if available. A picture of a policeman.

Concept: We can count on the authority of Christ and the integrity of his message.

Text: *John 5:43* (TEV) "I have come with my Father's authority...."

A policeman's badge is a symbol of authority. To become a member of the police force, one must pass certain tests that measure an individual's ability to be a part of a police team.

When the tests have been successfully completed, the trainee must attend classes and learn about the job. He or she must also receive physical training in order to become quick and skillful at certain procedures. Police work is difficult and demands high standards from those involved. After the training has been completed the trainee graduates and may begin a job as a policeman or policewoman.

Our law enforcement people are hired to protect others and enforce the laws. They have been given the authority to keep order in our communities. We can call on them if we have problems or need assistance. They are available for emergency situations. Sometimes they must deal with lawbreakers sternly. They must use their authority or power to stop people from doing something they shouldn't.

When Jesus lived on earth he told the people, "I have come with my Father's authority." He came to earth as a man with the authority of God. He had the greatest authority possible. What he said was truthful, just, and fair because it came from God.

We can look to him for help and protection. He is available in emergency situations. If we do something we shouldn't, he judges fairly. He is able to forgive us if we ask him.

Because of the nature of Christ, his laws are laws of love and power. His plan is one of law and order. We need only to believe in Christ's authority as the Son of God.

32

Open Up

Object: A budded branch or a flower that is in bud. A leaf or an opened flower.

Concept: Like buds responding to sunlight, we should open up to God's love.

Text: *Ephesians 1:18* (TEV) "I ask that your minds may be opened to see his light, so that you will know what is the hope to which he has called you, how rich are the wonderful blessings he promises his people, and how very great is his power at work in us who believe."

Have you ever run your hand along a branch of a tree or the stem of a plant and felt a tiny lump just under the surface? This lump is a bud and it contains an undeveloped leaf or flower. The bud is protected by scales. When the weather gets warmer, the bud begins to swell, the scales fall away, and a new leaf or flower emerges.

If we could look inside a leaf bud before it opens we would find a tightly folded leaf. It would be folded perfectly so that the center vein that carries food and water would not be crushed. Some leaves are tightly curled lengthwise, some are rolled from both sides to the center, and others are fan-folded.

Buds are like a promise. We see this miracle many times in the spring of the year. At first nothing is visible because the bud is hidden within the tree or plant. But as the days get longer, the bud responds to the light by expanding. The leaf or flower inside the bud grows and continues to develop. When the time is right, the bud opens and a beautiful leaf or flower unfolds.

In the Bible a prayer by the apostle Paul is recorded in this way: "I ask that your minds may be opened to see his light, so that you will know what is the hope to which he has called you, how rich are the wonderful blessings he promises his people, and how very great is his power at work in us who believe."

We are in many ways like a bud. We have special talents and abilities within us that are like promises. We have been given minds to make discoveries about God, ourselves, our world, and others. If we open our minds to God's light, many things are possible. When we respond to his love we grow, develop, and expand. His love is powerful. Let your life unfold with the light of God's love so that others can see and enjoy your beauty.

33

Tune In

Object: A portable radio.

Concept: We need to "tune in" to the Bible to enjoy its benefits.

Text: *1 Peter 1:25* (TEV) " '. . . but the word of the Lord remains forever.' This word is the Good News that was proclaimed to you."

This portable radio is easy for me to take along any-where I go. All I have to do is turn a knob and the radio waves are available for me to use. By turning another knob I have a choice of programs.

If my family is planning a picnic for tomorrow, I can listen to a weather report and find out if we might have rain. Or, I can turn on a news report and find out what is happening in other parts of the world. The radio brings us closer to other people by giving us information about how they live.

In an emergency such as a fire, snowstorm, or freeway accident, a radio tells us what is happening and what to do to protect ourselves and others.

Sometimes when people feel lonely they turn on the radio to hear voices and have company. Or if they are feeling happy, some people enjoy listening to cheerful music; the radio can provide that also.

We can use the Bible in much the same way that we use a radio. We can tune in to the very things we need. The Bible gives us many choices.

Some parts tells us what to expect in the future. Those verses are similar to the radio's weather report.

The Bible is written for all people everywhere. Everyone can understand it because underneath, everyone is alike. The Bible helps us to understand how others who may be different from us on the outside are actually very much like us on the inside.

If we have an emergency in our lives, the Bible is a good place to find out what is happening and what to do about the problem.

When we are feeling lonely we can read in the Bible about God's love and know we have a friend. And during the times we feel happy the verses that praise God help us to give thanks.

Like a portable radio, a Bible is easy to take with us anywhere we go. Just as we must turn on the radio to make it work for us, we must also tune in to the Bible to enjoy its benefits.

A radio sometimes develops static, making it difficult for us to hear the program. Occasionally, the power may go off or the batteries may go dead and we can't use the radio at all.

This is how a radio and the Bible are different. First Peter 1:25 states, "but the word of the Lord remains forever." The power of the Bible will always be available to us.

When we tune in to God's message we can always expect another exciting episode. It's Good News!

34

Wonderful! Wonderful!

Object: Picture of a beaver. Objects to touch, taste, smell, etc.

Concept: We can enjoy God's wonderful creation.

Text: *Isaiah 43:7* (TEV) "They are my own people, and I created them to bring me glory."

Our world is full of wonderful things, all created by God. One of the most remarkable animals he created is the beaver. This animal is perfectly designed for the world in which it lives and for the work it does.

As most of you probably know, beavers build dams and spend a great amount of time in the water. To keep warm they have a plump body and two fur coats. The inner coat is soft and thick for warmth. The fur of the outer coat is longer and waterproof.

The beaver has front paws that are small and nimble. He can use his paws to expertly maneuver sticks, rocks, and mud when building a dam. The large hind feet are webbed to help him swim well. The strong front teeth of a beaver are used for cutting down trees.

The beaver is an excellent underwater swimmer. His ears and nose have special valves to keep out the water and his eyelids are transparent so he can see while submerged. He can stay under the water for as long as fifteen minutes before he needs to surface.

A broad, flat tail is used as a prop when the beaver sits or stands and as a rudder when he swims. The tail is also used to slap the water loudly, warning the other beavers of danger.

Our human bodies are also wondrously made by God. We have keen eyesight to enjoy sunsets and snowflakes, tiny wildflowers, books, and smiles.

Our ears allow us to hear many sounds: ocean waves, a barking dog, church bells, music, and laughter.

With our nose we can smell bacon cooking, roses, bread baking in the oven, and a campfire.

Our sense of taste is special because we can enjoy ice cream, dill pickles, peanut butter, and strawberries. Can you think of other examples?

Our sense of touch brings many experiences to us. We can feel the softness of a baby's skin, the roughness of cement, the wetness of a creek, the warmth of the sun, and the coldness of an ice cube.

God created us and the world for his glory. One way we can honor God is to enjoy what he has given us. Take time to use your sense of sight, hearing, taste, touch, and smell to enjoy your surroundings. And don't forget to thank God for all his wonderful creations.

35
Grow Up

Object: A block of wood that demonstrates grain or growth lines.

Concept: Spiritual nourishment will keep us growing in Christ.

Text: *2 Peter 3:18* (TEV) "But continue to grow in the grace and knowledge of our Lord and Savior Jesus Christ. To him be the glory, now and forever! Amen."

A block of wood is something that has been taken from a living, growing tree. If you examine the wood closely, you will see that it has lines running through it. These lines are called the grain. The grain that is seen in wood is the tree's *growth* lines. Every year a tree has periods of growth. In spring, as the tree grows, it forms soft wood. In summer, the growth forms hard wood. The variation during these two periods of growth causes lines or rings to form. If you were to examine the trunk of a tree after it has been cut down, you could find out the age of the tree by counting the number of rings. In the autumn and winter seasons the sap, or tree food, goes out of a tree and the tree doesn't grow during that time. When that happens we say that the tree is dormant.

Let's talk about how people grow. We know that children grow into adults. The Bible teaches us about another kind of growth. "Continue to grow in the grace and knowledge of our Lord and Savior Jesus Christ." As our physical bodies grow we also need to increase our understanding about God, ourselves, and others. We can do that by reading the Bible and talking with teachers and friends about the things we don't understand.

If we have good information we can make better choices. The information we receive can be thought of as sap, or tree food. It is food that supplies us with the nourishment necessary for growing. People don't need to have dormant periods like trees have. We can continue to grow all year long. If we are inquisitive and search for answers, our knowledge will increase and we will grow.

This type of growth can continue all through our life, even when we are adults. The Bible encourages us to "continue to grow." When we "continue to grow in the grace and knowledge of our Lord," we experience God's love and become strong, hardy Christians.

36
Symbol of Love

Object: Hats of all types. A cross.

Concept: The cross is a symbol of what Christ has done for us.

Text: *Colossians 2:14* (TEV) "He cancelled the unfavorable record of our debts ... and did away with it completely by nailing it to the cross."

Let's talk about hats! Can you think of people who wear hats? Can you describe the type of hats they wear? Bus driver. Pilot. Skier. Nurse. Baseball player. Businessman. Cook. Gardener. Railroad engineer. Policeman. Sailor.

Often the hats people wear serve a purpose. The hat may keep a person warm, shade someone from the sun, or keep one's hair from blowing around. Sometimes hats are worn just for fun.

A hat may be a symbol of the work a person does. Sometimes we can identify a person's occupation by noticing what type of hat that person is wearing.

As Christians we have a symbol that we think about, especially during the Easter season. Do you know what it is? The cross. Jesus Christ died on a cross many years ago and because he was God's Son, three days later he was restored to life. Because of his sacrifice, all of us are offered the gift of eternal life. For a person who has faith in Christ, the cross is a symbol of hope. The cross reminds us of the work that Jesus did while he was on earth. It also reminds us of his continuing work, which is accomplished through us when we accept his love.

Since Christ is identified with the cross, some people wear a cross around their neck to identify themselves as Christians. We often see a cross on the roof of a church and sometimes inside the church as well. The cross identifies the church as a place to worship and learn about Jesus Christ. The Bible tells us that "he canceled the unfavorable record of our debts ... and did away with it completely by nailing it to the cross."

37

Always the Same

Object: A picture of a chameleon. A multicolored leaf.
Colored paper (green, yellow, cream, or brown).

Concept: God's love is unchangeable.

Text: *Malachi 3:6* "I the Lord do not change."

A chameleon is a very strange creature. It has rough,
scaly skin and horns protruding from its cone-shaped
head. Its neck is so short that it cannot turn its head.
The eyes are large and can move independently of each
other. A chameleon can look forward and backward at
the same time!

This strange creature also has a sticky tongue longer
than its entire body. In a third of a second, the tongue
can dart out and catch an insect.

Each leg of the chameleon has two sets of toes. One
set points ahead and the other points behind. The toes
and a special tail are used to grasp the branches of trees
where the lizard makes his home.

The most unusual thing about the chameleon is that
its skin can change color. When a chameleon is fright-
ened, or if there is a temperature variation, the lizard's
skin color will change, often matching its surrounding

environment. Sometimes the color pattern may resemble the colors of a blotchy leaf.

If you had a chance to see a chameleon you would not know what to expect. It could be green, yellow, cream, or brown. The next time you saw the chameleon it might be a different color. You might not be able to spot it at all if the colors were similar to the branch on which the lizard was resting. It could be very confusing.

It is fun to think about some of the strange creatures in God's world, and in doing so we can learn more about God.

In the Bible an Old Testament verse states, "I the Lord do not change." Another verse in the New Testament is similar: "Jesus Christ is the same yesterday and today and forever." Those verses tell us that with God we know what to expect. He has said that he loves us and that he will continue to love us no matter what happens. He will love us the same yesterday, today, and forever. We don't need to worry that we won't be able to find him because he will always be the same.

The chameleon is amazing because it is so changeable. God's love is even more amazing because it is unchangeable!

Suggestion: If you are able to obtain a live chameleon, reword the lesson accordingly.

38

A Proclamation

Object: Bumper sticker(s) or a picture of a car.

Concept: Knowing God is worth proclaiming.

Text: *Psalm 105:1* (TEV) "Give thanks to the LORD, proclaim his greatness; tell the nations what he has done."

As you ride in a car or bus along the freeway, you may notice a curious thing. Some of the cars that pass by have signs on their bumpers. These signs are called bumper stickers and people use them to tell others about something they feel is important or exciting. Bumper stickers are used to give a personal message to the world. That message is usually short, clear, and easy to understand. We could call the message that is printed on a bumper sticker a proclamation.

Let's talk about some of the things that people like to share with the world by putting messages on the bumpers of their cars. Sometimes grandparents want others to know how happy they are to have grandchildren. If a person is proud to be a member of a certain club or organization, he may say so on a bumper sticker. People may proclaim their nationality in the same way. Perhaps a person's occupation or hobby is what they want to share with others. Some bumper stickers are used to make people laugh. Others remind us of safety rules. The messages found on bumper stickers are many.

Whatever a bumper sticker might declare, the purpose is the same: it is a way of reaching others. It is a way of saying, "Look world, I have something important and exciting to share. Pay attention!"

The psalmist in the Old Testament tells us that we should "Give thanks to the Lord, proclaim His greatness; tell the nations what He has done."

God has given us many reasons to be thankful. If we take the time to look at the world in which we live we will find miracles all around us. The beauty of what God has created is evident in many ways. The trees, clouds, rivers, mountains, flowers, rain, and sunshine are all part of his greatness.

God's most wonderful gift is the love he gave to us through his Son, Jesus Christ. We see God's love not only in the beauty of creation, but also in the privilege of knowing him in a personal way through Jesus Christ. We have much to be excited and happy about.

We don't need a bumper sticker to tell others about God. If we try to live our lives according to the example Christ set for us, others will be able to see the important and exciting message of God's love. His love will flow through us and reach others. Our lives can *proclaim* his greatness and "tell the nations what He has done."

39

Be Comfortable

Object: Pillow; pillowcase; feathers or stuffing.

Concept: God gives us peace as we learn about his love.

Text: *John 14:27* (TEV) "Peace is what I leave with you; it is my own peace that I give you. I do not give it as the world does. Do not be worried and upset; do not be afraid."

D o you use a pillow on your bed at night? Why? A pillow is soft. It supports your head. It makes you more comfortable. It feels good. Just thinking about a pillow can make you want to take a nap, can't it? A good pillow adds to the restful feeling we need to have for falling asleep.

Some people like a high, firm pillow. Others prefer a soft, squishy pillow. It seems as though everyone likes their own pillow the best.

Let's talk about how a pillow is constructed. A pillow is a piece of cloth that has been stitched into a rectangle and stuffed with feathers, down, foam, or a man-made batting. It is the substance inside that makes the pillow soft and comfortable. A pillow might have a pretty pillowcase over it to keep it clean, but it is the stuffing that is important. If a pillow didn't have stuffing it would just be a limp piece of cloth. It wouldn't be useful or comfortable.

At church we hear our teachers, pastor, and friends talk about peace. The reason people talk about peace so much is because it is important. Everyone wants to feel peaceful. The word *peace* is also used many times in the Bible. Do you know what it means?

When we talk about the world, peace means the absence of war. It means that people have found ways to "get along" with each other.

When we define peace for ourselves, we call it "peace of mind." Peace of mind means that we feel comfortable, happy, and content. It is the absence of arguments, worry, or fear.

God has given us a gift and that gift is peace of mind and heart. He has sent the Holy Spirit to teach us the important things we need to know to feel peaceful. The Holy Spirit, who is part of God, helps us learn how to love God, ourselves, and others. The peace of God comes from the love of God that is inside you. Just like the stuffing in a pillow, it is the love inside you that is important, comfortable, and useful. The more we learn about God's love the more peaceful we will feel.

Tonight when you lie down to go to sleep and feel the comfort of your pillow, think about the comfort of the Holy Spirit and the peace that can be yours by accepting God's gift.

40
Wonders of the World

Object: Picture(s) of the Grand Canyon. Map of the United States. Vacation supplies.

Concept: There are many marvelous wonders in God's creation for us to enjoy.

Text: *Psalm 65:8* (TEV) "The whole world stands in awe of the great things that you have done."

The Grand Canyon, in the northwest part of Arizona, is one of the seven natural wonders of the world. The Colorado River runs through the canyon which is eighteen miles wide at its widest part and a mile deep in some places.

The huge canyon was formed over many, many years by erosion from the river, rain, wind, and snow.

The layers of rock that form the walls of the canyon are different colors and shades. Millions of people visit the Grand Canyon each year to enjoy its beauty.

There are several trails that lead to the bottom of the Grand Canyon; tourists can hike these or ride down them on mules to explore the gorge. The canyon is so deep that the temperature can be twenty-five degrees warmer on the bottom than it is at the top.

Although the Grand Canyon is awesome and beautiful

there are many other things in God's world to explore and appreciate.

We read in the Bible that, "The whole world stands in awe of the great things that you have done." We should think about what God has provided for our pleasure and enjoy those things. Take time to look at the stars, smell a flower, feel a soft breeze on your skin, taste an apple, and listen to the rain. The marvels of creation are all around us. We can be thankful and praise God for the great things he has done.

God's world contains many wonders from the huge Grand Canyon to a tiny seashell. Explore God's world and enjoy the good things that you find.

41
Hit the Target

Object: Bow, arrow, target.

Concept: We need to aim for the bull's eye: love.

Text: *1 Corinthians 14:1* (TEV) "It is love, then, that you should strive for."

Archery, the use of a bow and arrow, is a sport enjoyed by many people. Although the Egyptians used bows and arrows over six thousand years ago for hunting and as a weapon against their enemies, in our country the bow and arrow is used mainly for fun. Archery is a sport in which the archer places the string of the bow into a slot in the end of the arrow. *(Demonstrate.)* He then lifts the bow into an upright position, and holding the arrow in place, pulls the string back toward his body. When he lets go of the string the arrow flies through the air.

Standing several yards from the archer is a target, a series of red, blue, black, and white circles. Exactly in the center is a gold-colored circle called a bull's eye.

Archers shoot arrows toward the target, making it their goal to come as close as possible to the bull's eye. They try to set the arrow on the right course. If their aim is accurate they will hit the bull's eye.

God wants us to plan our lives with some direction. Our lives will be more happy and successful if we have a goal to strive for. The Bible gives us good advice for setting our lives on the right course: "It is love, then, that you should strive for" (1 Cor. 14:1).

We have many choices to make as we grow. Choices are like circles on a target. There are many, but the closer we get to the center, which is love, the happier we will be. We don't always hit the target, but as we practice becoming more loving we will get closer to the bull's eye, God's love. We can set our course and aim toward love!

Suggestion: To illustrate the concept, place the word *love* in the bull's eye.

42

Turn Over

Object: Cooked and half-cooked pancakes. A box of pancake mix. A recipe book. A Bible.

Concept: We need to turn our lives over to God.

Text: *Psalm 22:27* (TEV) "All nations will remember the Lord. From every part of the world they will turn to him; all races will worship him."

$\mathbf{D}$o you eat pancakes for breakfast? They taste good, especially with butter added and syrup poured over the top.

Let's talk about how to make pancakes. For the best results we should follow a recipe that gives good directions about what ingredients to use and how to put them together. This particular recipe has the following directions:

Beat well — 1 egg

Stir in — 1¼ cups of milk

Beat in — 1¼ cups flour, 1 teaspoon sugar, 2 tablespoons shortening, 1½ teaspoons baking powder, and ½ teaspoon salt

Do you know what to do next? Heat a frying pan to

the right temperature and pour the right amount of batter into the pan. We can tell the pancakes are cooking when small bubbles begin to form. What should we do then? We need to turn the pancake over with a spatula so the other side can cook. If we didn't turn it over, the pancake would be doughy on the top and too brown on the bottom. *(Show them half-cooked pancakes.)* It wouldn't be good to eat.

We must follow the *directions* carefully in order to make good pancakes and one of the most important steps is to turn the pancake over.

There are good directions in the Bible to improve our lives. If we study the directions carefully we will find that we must turn our lives over to God for the best results. How can we do that? By asking to be forgiven for the mistakes we have made and by being willing to accept his love. If we try to live without his help, our lives will be like the pancake that has been cooked on only one side. We won't be complete.

Follow the directions in the Bible and turn your life over to God. Then you will be well-done!

Suggestion: This lesson could be expanded to allow the children to make and eat pancakes.

43

Solid as a Rock

Object: Rocks of various sizes, shapes, and colors.

Concept: People are like rocks; God is "a Rock."

Text: *2 Samuel 22:47* "The Lord lives! Praise be to my Rock! Exalted be God, the Rock, my Savior!"

Everyone has seen or touched a rock. They are ordinary and common but they also can be useful, beautiful, and fun. Have you ever compared rocks to people? Some are sharp, others smooth. They can be large or small and can be many different colors.

While you examine this collection of rocks *(pass them around)*, let's see what other interesting things we can discover.

Beautiful mountains are made of rocks. Did you know that under the layer of soil, the whole crust of the earth is made of rock? In what other ways are rocks useful? Rocks are used to build houses and roads. They make good foundations and give support.

There are people who are like useful rocks. They are strong and do the work that needs to be done. They are the helpers and builders who give support to their families, friends, church, and community.

Rocks are beautiful. At the beach some of the rocks have been washed by the water and polished by the sand until they are smooth and shiny. Some people like to polish rocks by putting them in a rock tumbler. Often rocks are made into lovely jewelry.

There are people who are like beautiful rocks. They have been polished by reading God's Word and living a Christian life. These beautiful people are necessary because they help us find God.

Rocks can be fun. Have you ever dropped pebbles into a creek, skipped a stone across a lake, or thrown rocks into the ocean? It's fun! Rocks can also be painted with many designs.

There are people who are fun to have as friends. They smile and laugh and make us feel happy. These people are necessary because they help us find joy in our world.

Rocks can also be a problem. We can stumble over them and fall. If a rock is thrown it can hit someone and hurt them.

Unfortunately, there are people who are like problem rocks. These people may do something to hurt others and make them fall. Or, they may say something unkind and that may hurt, just like a rock that is thrown.

Rocks are such an important part of our world that the Bible uses the word *rock* to describe God. "The Lord lives! Praise be to my Rock! Exalted be God, the Rock, my Savior!"

When you see a rock, think about how useful, beautiful, and fun they can be. Our lives can be useful, beautiful, and fun if we center ourselves on "the Rock, our Savior!"

44
Who Cares?

Object: Fresh or canned pineapple.

Concept: God cares for us.

Text: *1 Peter 5:7* (TEV) "Leave all your worries with him, because he cares for you."

This fresh pineapple is special—sweet, juicy, and delicious. I'll cut it into pieces so you can taste it. *(Cut and distribute.)*

Much care is needed to produce a beautiful fruit like this. Pineapples must be grown in the proper location. They do well in an area where there is a low rainfall. They need loose, well-drained, acid soil. In Hawaii, where pineapples grow, the soil is red because it is rich in iron.

The soil must be cultivated to get rid of weeds. Then, heavy mulch paper is laid over the soil to keep weeds from growing and also to hold moisture in the soil. Holes are punched through the paper and pineapple shoots are planted through the holes. The soil must be treated to control pests that would bother the plant and the plant is also sprayed to remove harmful insects. Pineapple growers do tests on the plants to determine what kind and how much plant food is needed. While it is growing, the pineapple plant must also have the right amount of water. It takes two years from the time a plant is put into the ground until a pineapple is formed and ready to eat.

As you can see, pineapples need much special care.

We receive our care from God. He has supplied a wonderful world for us to enjoy. He provides our food, rain, and sunshine. He has given us parents to protect and teach us. God comforts us and helps us with our problems. He is constantly watching over us. He is concerned that we grow up to be the best person that we can possibly be. Like the pineapple, God wants us to be beautiful and useful.

Pineapple growers spend two years caring for a plant so that it will produce a pineapple. God cares for us forever!

45
The Right Direction

Object: U.S., state, and city maps.

Concept: The Bible is our road map through life.

Text: *Hebrews 13:5* (TEV) "For God has said, 'I will never leave you; I will never abandon you.'"

Have you ever gone to an unfamiliar city with your family and had trouble finding your way around its streets? When people travel in an unfamiliar place, they usually need information to help them find their way. A map of the city you're visiting can be very helpful. It will show you how to get from one place to another, it labels the streets and indicates their length, and it reveals where parks, lakes, and certain buildings are.

For longer trips a map of a certain state or a United States map may be needed. That kind of map will show you where freeways, rivers, lakes, mountains, towns, and cities are located. Railroad tracks, airports, points of interest, and national parks might also be shown. It will tell you the elevation of the mountains and the distance between two places. Can you think of other information you can find on a map?

Maps are valuable when used as a guide because they help us get to where we want to go and show us what to expect along the way. A map also reveals obstacles that might block our path. By studying the map we can find the best way to get around those obstacles. Maps keep us from getting lost if we use the information and make good choices.

The Bible states, "For God has said, 'I will never leave you; I will never abandon you.'" That promise tells us that we always have help available to us. The Bible is a guide for our lives just as a road map guides us when we travel. It helps us get to where we want to go and shows us what to expect along the way. It outlines the steps a person must take to accept God's love and lead a more satisfying, useful life. It warns us of problems we might encounter and gives suggestions for how to handle those problems. God is with us at all times and speaks to us through his Word, the Bible. When we encounter an obstacle, we can search the Bible for directions and pray for guidance. When we use the information it provides, the Bible helps us find our way and keeps us from feeling lost.

A road map is a helpful, necessary guide when traveling in an unfamiliar place. The Bible, too, is a good traveling companion!

46
Strength of a Horse

Object: A picture of horses.

Concept: We grow stronger as we learn about God and his ways.

Text: *Psalm 118:14* (TEV) "The Lord makes me powerful and strong; he has saved me."

We usually think of the horse as being strong-legged, but when it is born it is actually quite a wobbly creature. Compared to the rest of its body, its legs are extremely long and very weak. Called a foal, the baby horse falls several times before it is able to stand. This awkwardness is necessary because it helps straighten and strengthen the legs. Within one to two hours after birth the foal, encouraged by its mother, is able to stand.

The first few days of a foal's life are spent resting and eating. All the while, the mother cares for and protects her baby. This is the way a foal grows and gains strength.

When a horse is full grown it weighs from nine hundred to twelve hundred pounds. Horses have great strength and stamina. They can carry a rider or a heavy load for many miles. Some horses are trained to race and can attain great speeds.

So, a once awkward, wobbly foal becomes a mighty animal of great strength.

Strength is not only a physical attribute but also spiritual. The Bible instructs us about this idea. "The Lord makes me powerful and strong; he has saved me." As we learn more about God and his ways, we become more sure of what we believe. That is called faith. By studying the Bible, praying, and being curious about the world around us, our faith develops.

At first we may feel awkward and weak, just like a newborn foal. There is much we don't understand and much to learn. As we struggle to grow and try out new ideas, we gain strength. We may make mistakes or fail but the Bible tells us that God understands our weaknesses. We are encouraged to try again, just as a foal must try several times before it is able to stand.

As God's children we are given encouragement, protection, and care so that we will grow into powerful, strong adults. The power we receive from God gives us inner strength so that we can take care of ourselves and others.

47

Two Peas in a Pod

Object: Fresh peas in the pod if available. A box of frozen peas. A can of peas.

Concept: God treats all his children with fairness and love.

Text: *Acts 10:34* (TEV) "Peter began to speak: 'I now realize that it is true that God treats everyone on the same basis.'"

Have you ever heard the phrase, "As alike as two peas in a pod?" If you opened a pea pod you might be surprised to see how similar the peas are. The peas are the same color, size, and shape. If we were to eat the peas the flavor would be the same. We would discover that all peas have the same fragrance. The similarity is remarkable.

Let's open a box of frozen peas and check to see if they are similar. *(Open box.)* They seem identical to each other. Now let's look into a container of canned peas. *(Open can.)* Can you see how much alike they are?

Perhaps we can learn something about God and his love by thinking about the similarities we find in peas. The Bible tells us that "God treats everyone on the same basis." His love is not based on our appearance, where we live, what we do or have done. Although we are all different in many ways, we are all treated with the same fairness and love. He treats us as individuals and loves us as if we were "as alike as two peas in a pod."

Every individual has the opportunity to become a part of God's family by believing in his Son, Jesus Christ. We all have the opportunity to be forgiven for past mistakes and receive his love. Even though we are unique people, we can realize as the disciple Peter did that God treats everyone on the same basis.

48

Purr-fect Peace

Object: A well-mannered cat (or a picture of a cat), cat food, and a cat toy.

Concept: Like a purring cat, we as God's children can be happy and content.

Text: *Romans 15:13* "May the God of hope fill you with all joy and peace as you trust in him, so that you may overflow with hope by the power of the Holy Spirit."

D oes anyone in our group have a cat for a pet? What do you like most about your cat? Is your cat playful? Loving?

Cats are interesting animals. They can be independent, playful, and lovable. They are excellent hunters and are useful because they keep rats and mice out of houses, barns, and warehouses.

Cats have strong, muscular bodies and a keen sense of hearing. They can see well at night and their whiskers help them move around in the dark without bumping into things.

If you look at a cat's paw, you will see that they have claws that they can retract. When they are playful they pull in their claws so they will not scratch their human friend.

Cats have a very distinct way of letting us know when

they are happy and content. They will rub against your leg or jump into your lap and make a purring sound. If you pet your cat it may purr loudly.

Enjoying a cat's purr can be a reminder to us that as children of God we too can be happy and content. When we trust God we receive the power of the Holy Spirit in our lives. That Spirit is one of love, hope, joy, and peace. By knowing that God loves us and that we have his love within us, we can continue to feel happiness and contentment. Trust in God allows us to have peace of mind, no matter what the circumstances.

When a cat is pleased it lets others know by making a purring sound. When we feel joy and peace we let others know by our cheerfulness, smiles, and helpfulness.

"May the God of hope fill you with all joy and peace as you trust in him, so that you may overflow with hope by the power of the Holy Spirit."

49
Touch the Sky

Object: A yardstick (for demonstrating how thick the bark of a sequoia is).

Concept: God's love is incredibly large.

Text: *Psalm 108:4* (TEV) "Your constant love reaches above the heavens; your faithfulness touches the skies."

One of the largest and oldest living things in our world is the giant sequoia. This tree, which grows to a height of over three hundred feet, has been on earth since long before the birth of Christ. It is believed that some of the giant sequoias are over four thousand years old! The bark is one to two feet thick and is resistant to forest fires and insects that might damage the tree.

The sequoias are found growing in groves on the slopes of the Sierra Nevada mountains in California. Many people travel there to view their beauty and awesome size. It is difficult to comprehend how huge the trees are, but if you can see in your mind how high a twenty-story building is, imagine that the sequoia is taller than that!

At it's base, the sequoia's trunk is bigger than the average living room. A bough from such a tree can be seventy feet long. Have you ever seen a tree so large?

It is interesting and fun to think about something as

big and wonderful as a sequoia. It is difficult to imagine their size.

In the Old Testament the psalmist tells us about something else that is big and high and which seems to touch the sky: God's love and faithfulness. "Your constant love reaches above the heavens," he writes. "Your faithfulness touches the skies."

Isn't it wonderful to think about God's great love for us? God's love for us is so great that we cannot measure it. It is larger than our understanding. It is so big that it goes beyond this world. Just as it is difficult to comprehend how big the sequoias are, *it is difficult to comprehend the size of God's love.*

Stand tall, like the giant sequoia. Don't limit your value or possibilities for growth. Enjoy the great proportions of God's love!

50
Respectfully Yours

Object: Pictures of a trillium or other wildflowers. A bouquet or corsage from a garden or floral shop.

Concept: Friends, like flowers, need to be treated with care and respect.

Text: *Romans 12:10* (TEV) "Love one another warmly as Christian brothers, and be eager to show respect for one another."

F lowers are one of God's best gifts to us. There are many different kinds of flowers and all are beautiful.

Some people like to grow flowers in a window box or in their garden. Flowers can be used in bouquets to make a home seem bright and cheerful. Often they are shared with friends.

Other flowers are grown in special gardens and sold to flower shops. These flowers can be purchased and given as gifts on special occasions. Flowers are also a nice way to cheer people who are ill.

A trillium, sometimes called the wild Easter lily, is a flower that should not be picked. It is a beautiful wildflower and grows in damp, shaded areas of the forest. When it blooms in the spring, it produces a single flower with three pure white petals surrounded by three bright green leaves. When this flower is picked, the leaves are also removed and the stalk has no way to make and store food. It may take several years before the trillium is able to bloom again.

Even though there are many flowers grown specifically for the purpose of making bouquets and corsages, certain wildflowers like the trillium should not be picked or disturbed. They must be treated with care and respect if we are to enjoy their beauty, year after year.

As we think about the trillium, perhaps we can learn something about friendship. Like flowers, friends are one of the most wonderful parts of our lives. The Bible teaches us about friendship. "Love one another warmly as Christian brothers," it instructs us, "and be eager to show respect for one another."

We should love and enjoy our friends but we also need to treat them with care and respect. Just as a trillium is a delicate flower, people have feelings that are delicate. If we are unkind we can hurt another person's feelings and it may take time before they will feel comfortable with us again. If we have hurt someone, whether we meant to or not, the best way to repair the damage we caused is to ask for forgiveness.

Flowers and friends are beautiful. Treat them with love and respect!